The Illuminated Introvert

Published by Giovanni Ricco

~~~~
~~~~

Content

Illuminated Introvert:
A Journey from Within

Forehead

Dive into the luminous world of the introvert, where every page is a beacon of insight waiting to be discovered. Rather than consuming this book in one go, let your intuition guide you. Skim the table of contents and let your heart gravitate towards the chapters that resonate deeply. As you immerse yourself, remember to apply the principles and exercises in your own life. Our inner compass doesn't always follow a linear path, and sometimes the most profound revelations emerge from the unexpected.

While the strategies presented have been transformative for many, they may not always align with your unique journey. Contexts evolve, and so do we. However, as you absorb these teachings, they'll find a way back to you, reshaped by your inner wisdom, ready to guide you when the time is right. Remember, no single approach is eternal, but by the end, you'll uncover timeless methods that have profoundly impacted the author's life.

Each chapter is adorned with a meticulously crafted image, a testament to the adage that a picture speaks a thousand words. These images, birthed from the fusion of artificial intelligence and the author's vision, are more than mere illustrations. They are windows into the soul of the chapter. Engage with them, and you'll find that the essence of each lesson becomes effortlessly etched in your mind. Welcome to "The Illuminated Introvert," where every image and word is a journey into the depths of introspection.

Introduction

Welcome, dear reader, to a book that has been carefully crafted from personal experience, introspection, and a sincere passion for understanding the intricacies of the introverted mind. This book, "The Illuminated Introvert," aims to delve into the depths of the introverted psyche, unravelling its mysteries and presenting ways to navigate its complexities.

As an introvert myself, I have experienced first-hand the challenges and struggles that come with this particular personality type. Introversion often leads us to spend extended periods in solitude, fostering a tendency to overthink and introspect. While this provides a unique perspective on life, it can simultaneously strain relationships and lead to feelings of being misunderstood. It's not uncommon for introverts to feel lonely and hopeless in a world that seems to revolve around extroverted norms.

However, it's crucial to realize that there is nothing inherently 'wrong' with being an introvert. Introverts form a minority in society, but that doesn't diminish their value. Nature, in its infinite wisdom, has selected a diversity of personality types, including introverts, to contribute to the evolution and progress of humanity.

Over the years, I've grappled with my introversion, often searching for a way to 'correct' this aspect of myself that seemed to cause suffering. In this journey, I've discovered a variety of methods that have helped me not only accept my introversion but also to thrive as an introvert. These strategies have brought me closer to a sense of harmony and happiness with my life and my relationships.

In this book, I intend to share these methods with you. However, I must clarify that there is no 'one-size-fits-all' approach to living as an introvert. Numerous books and resources offer myriad strategies, but their effectiveness often varies depending on individual circumstances and contexts.

What I aim to offer in these pages are the methods that have proven most successful for me after numerous trials and iterations over the years. While they might not be universally applicable, they are rooted in personal experience and have been fine-tuned for the introverted mind.

"The Illuminated Introvert" is a testament to the unique challenges and triumphs of the introverted journey. I hope it provides you with insights, strategies, and, most importantly, a sense of comfort in knowing that you are not alone in your experiences. Remember, being an introvert is not a flaw to be fixed, but a trait to be understood, embraced, and celebrated.

Understanding Our Personalities: The Four Character Types and Their Interactions

In our diverse society, it's common to observe a wide range of personalities. Each person has a unique set of characteristics that make them who they are, yet many of us exhibit traits that fall into one of four primary personality types: the Analytical, the Driver, the Amiable, and the Expressive.

The Analytical individuals are deep thinkers, setting high standards for themselves and others. They are known for their organized nature, methodical approach, and perfectionism. However, they can sometimes be overly critical, moody, and may over-analyse situations, causing decision-making to be a challenging task.

Drivers are dynamic and assertive. They possess natural leadership qualities, are goal-oriented, and are exceptionally determined. Their visionary mindset enables them to see the 'big picture,' yet they may overlook the finer details. Drivers' confidence can sometimes come across as insensitivity or arrogance, and they are prone to making hasty decisions without fully considering the implications.

Amiable personalities are typically friendly, pleasant, and patient. They have a balanced disposition, valuing harmony and avoiding conflict. They're diplomatic and calm but can sometimes appear passive or stubborn due to their aversion to confrontation.

Expressive are social butterflies. They are outgoing, ambitious, charismatic, and persuasive, often turning difficult situations into humorous ones. Their energy can be infectious, but they can also come off as disorganized, undisciplined, and excessively talkative.

Understanding these personality types is essential because it gives us insight into why we behave the way we do. However, it is crucial to recognize that these types are not rigid categories that we neatly fit into. In reality, our personalities lie along a continuum, with each of us exhibiting traits from multiple personality types.

In many cases, we have a dominant character type that is most apparent in our behaviour, while another type may be more latent, influencing our actions in subtler ways. For instance, a person might be predominantly Analytical but also have latent Amiable tendencies, leading them to be highly organized and meticulous but also peace-loving and empathetic. This blend of dominant and latent character types shapes our behaviour and interactions, contributing to the richness of our personalities.

Recognizing and understanding our personality types is not merely an exercise in self-understanding; it also fosters a sense of empathy and acceptance for others and ourselves. We must remember that there is no superior or inferior personality type, and success is not exclusive to any one type.

It's essential to appreciate that you are not an anomaly. You are not alone in your feelings, thoughts, and behaviours; there are others who share your personality type. You are just one variation of the human being, and that in itself is beautiful.

It's easy to look at successful people who are vastly different from us and feel inadequate. However, it's crucial to remember that there's nothing wrong with being who you are. Your value does not decrease because of someone else's success. You have unique strengths and potential that align with your character type, and it's important to recognize and nurture them.

Striving to be something we're not often leads to stress and dissatisfaction. Accepting ourselves as we are, understanding our strengths and areas for growth, and striving for personal improvement rather than imitation is the path to genuine fulfilment and success.

So, remember, it's okay to be you. You are a vital part of this world's diverse tapestry, and your unique personality contributes to its richness and vibrancy. Embrace your personality type and use it as a tool to understand yourself better and navigate the world around you. After all, then you need to make sure that my article is consistent with the latest studies and researches.

The Limits of Words: Understanding the Connection Between High and Low-Level Mental Programming

The connection between high and low-level mental programming can be readily exemplified through the limits of words. A word or a phrase can have a profound emotional impact on you. However, this impact inevitably diminishes over time because the same word or phrase no longer stimulates the same emotion, nor does it do so with the same intensity. Therefore, it's inevitable that we can never be permanently tied to a concept simply because it's no longer connected to the original emotion.

Words, in themselves, are empty vessels. It is we who associate them with emotions, and being emotional beings, a word is by no means a guarantee of emotional coherence and stability. This phenomenon highlights the fluidity of our emotional responses and the transient nature of our associations with words.

The solution to this transient nature of emotional association is simple: we must find another word that elicits the same emotion. This practice is a form of mental reprogramming, where we consciously search for new linguistic associations to maintain the desired emotional state.

It's important to note that while I've used words as an example, this concept extends to all elements that we associate with an emotion, such as music. A song that once stirred strong emotions and was highly enjoyable may lose its effectiveness over time. The connection fades, the emotions associated with it wane, and it no longer holds the same emotional potency.

This process underlines the dynamic nature of our emotional responses and the continuous changes in our mental programming. It is a testament to the adaptability of the human mind and its capacity to form, reform, and sever connections based on our emotional responses.

Understanding this, we can appreciate the importance of continually cultivating our mental garden. We must actively seek new associations and stimuli to nourish our emotional well-being, all while understanding that change and transience are integral parts of this process.

The Multi-layered Mind: Understanding Mental and Physical Practices for Holistic Well-being

Every method, procedure, and control mechanism we employ for personal management has significant high-level mental implications. It's important to notice that a mental concept's effect can vary over time. This variability is because it's tied to countless internal (subconscious) and external factors, most of which are beyond our control. It's not possible to have a 'permanent centre of gravity' under these conditions. The system - the mind - is not designed for that.

We may apply specific methodologies in precise internal and external domains, and they may be useful only in 'cycles' when the same conditions reoccur. This concept may not seem novel; it may even appear obvious to some.

So, what methodologies can work consistently? The answer resides in those at a lower level: bodily actions such as eating, walking, exercising. These are lower-level activities with a less intense mental involvement. This realization underpins methodologies such as yoga and similar practices that focus on breathing and meditation.

There may come a point when it seems like these methods aren't working, but they are the ones worth persisting with. Always and in all their variations, these practices can help you achieve what you truly desire: total happiness.

The key lies in developing low and very low-level methodologies that bypass the involvement of the higher, more unstable mind. This strategy aligns with the understanding that the mind is a high-level tool. Like all tools, it should be used correctly. It's worth noting that the mind is flexible, creating sub-tools depending on the situation.

Classifying methods at various levels from highest to lowest can provide clarity in this realm. For now, we'll focus on those at the lower level.

At the highest level, we have intellectual pursuits and complex problem-solving tasks, which require deep cognitive processing and high mental involvement. Then, we find activities like reading, writing, or studying, which still require significant cognitive effort but are more routine.

Moving to the mid-level, we find activities that require mental focus but less cognitive processing, such as playing an instrument or cooking a familiar recipe.

At the lower level are more automatic, habituated tasks like brushing your teeth or tying your shoelaces. These activities require minimal cognitive engagement, allowing the mind to relax or wander.

At the very lowest level are fundamental body actions: breathing, blinking, walking. These activities are largely subconscious and automatic, and mindfulness practices often focus on these tasks to develop awareness and presence.

Understanding the diverse nature of these methodologies and how they impact our mental and physical well-being can provide a holistic approach to personal management. It emphasizes the need to balance our mental exertions with lower-level bodily actions, providing a road map for sustainable health and happiness.

Remember, the mind is a high-level tool. Like all tools, it should be used in the correct way. Note that the mind is flexible, creating sub-tools according to different situations. This adaptability is its strength, and knowing how to harness it can be the key to a balanced and fulfilling life.

High-Level Mental Programming: Suggestions to the Unconscious

The term 'mental programming' may not entirely capture the essence of what we are trying to accomplish here. In essence, what we are doing is making suggestions to the unconscious mind. However, the effect is very much like programming oneself as if programming a computer.

Our minds function like computers, yet they operate differently from the digital computers we are accustomed to. The mind is comprised of multiple layers, many of which are not directly accessible to us. We cannot fully see or understand them, yet they govern us. However, we can suggest to them how to behave.

To make this suggestion, we need to be in a state of calm. Therefore, it's recommended to use this method in conjunction with a low-level method. Solitude, calm, and an open and relaxing environment amplify communication with the subconscious, enabling us to proceed with the suggestion (refer to the Low-Level section for more details).

The method described here is quite simple yet effective. It requires repeating the suggestion in a rhythmic manner over an extended period. It's important to note that the suggestion should not be imposing. The mind rejects impositions but accepts suggestions that align with its personality. Therefore, it's crucial to not only know which suggestion to give for which purpose but also how to give it.

The terms for programming should not be many. You can select them based on your needs. Here is a list of terms against situations:

- Anxiety: 'I know what to do!' Anxiety stems from uncertainty about the future and how to face it. By programming and reiterating that you'll be ready, your heart becomes hard and strong, and anxiety vanishes.

- Sadness: 'Surprise me!' Sadness often stems from a lack of novelty; a present that always seems the same eventually leads to depression. By focusing on what surprises you, whether it comes from you or your environment, your mood will improve, and you'll begin to appreciate even the smallest things because they surprise you.

Remember, the terms for programming should not feel like impositions. They should be set as proposals or suggestions, as if you were speaking to another person. This approach ensures that the process feels natural and conducive to your personal growth.

By implementing this high-level mental programming, we can direct our unconscious mind towards desired behaviours and attitudes. Like a subtle whisper in the wind, these suggestions can influence our subconscious, guiding us towards achieving our most profound goals and aspirations.

Illuminating the Introvert's Subconscious: A Voyage Into the Depths of Self

Introduction

Introversion is often associated with a rich inner life, one that is teeming with thoughts, feelings, and reflections. These inner experiences are tied to the subconscious, a vast reservoir of memories, emotions, and impulses that significantly influence our behaviour, perceptions, and personality. This article aims to use a metaphorical exploration to illuminate the nature of the introverted subconscious and suggest ways of engaging with it.

The Subconscious as a Pool

Imagine standing naked on the edge of a circular pool, filled with black water. The diameter of the pool is equal to your height. This ring of water is merely the surface of the pool, which extends beneath the pavement and into unseen depths. Around you, it's pitch dark, obscuring your surroundings and making the pool's surface the only thing you can clearly perceive.

This pool is your subconscious. Its surface represents your current state of mind, reflecting your thoughts and feelings. The waves on the surface of the pool are representative of the state of your subconscious. If the waves are tall and frequent, it indicates that your subconscious is in a state of alertness or anxiety. Conversely, if the waves are small and infrequent, it suggests that your subconscious is calm and tranquil.

Engaging with the Subconscious

Within the depths of this pool are objects and figures - memories, desires, fears, and aspects of your personality - swimming or floating closer to the surface. They're not immediately accessible, but they are visible if you look carefully. These are elements of your subconscious that may be influencing your thoughts, feelings, and behaviour without you fully realizing it.

Interacting with your subconscious should be approached with care. Diving headfirst into this pool can lead to confusion or distress, as it could overwhelm you with unprocessed emotions or forgotten memories. Instead, think of reaching out gently with your hand, just below the surface of the water, brushing against what lies beneath. This gesture represents conscious engagement with your subconscious, a respectful inquiry into its depths.

This metaphorical interaction with your subconscious can be actualized through techniques such as meditation, mindfulness, self-reflection, and even professional therapy. These activities encourage gentle exploration of your subconscious mind, helping you understand your thoughts, emotions, and responses better.

Conclusion

For introverts, understanding the subconscious can be a key part of self-discovery and personal growth. The pool metaphor provides a vivid visual aid to conceptualize the subconscious and its dynamics. By learning to observe and gently interact with your subconscious, you can gain deeper insights into your inner world, fostering self-awareness and self-acceptance. Remember, the exploration of your subconscious is a personal journey, one that unfolds at your own pace, in your own time.

As you stand at the edge of your subconscious pool, remember: every ripple, every wave, every submerged figure, is a part of you. Embrace this complex inner landscape and celebrate its depth and richness. After all, it's these depths that often give introverts their unique perspective and creative potential.

Breathing into Being: A Path to Higher-Level Mental Programming

Our journey begins in front of the verdant expanses. Stand tall, feet planted firmly on the ground, eyes barely open, taking in the majesty of life pulsating around you.

Now, begin counting deep breaths. Each breath is an affirmation of life, a testament to your presence in the here and now. Allow your focus to centre on your breathing, on what you see, and what you feel in your present moment. Banish or reduce every thought, allowing your mind to enter a state of tranquil clarity.

Count at least up to 30 breaths before you finish. Each breath is a step towards deeper mindfulness, a step closer to the core of your being.

Once you've completed the 30 breaths, you may choose to continue with phrases of mental programming (high-level methods), synchronized with your breath. For example, the phrase 'I can do it.' This form of mental programming forms the cornerstone of our high-level method discussed in the 'Mental Programming' section.

A few notes to consider during this process:

Strive for spiritual 'Suspension', a state of unity with the heavens and the earth, timeless and spaceless.

Your breath should be consciously deep, demanding more attention from your mind.

Visualize your lungs working, engaging in every part involved in the process of breathing.

The terms for programming should not be many; you can select them based on your needs. Here is a list of terms against situations:

For Anxiety, use the term: 'I know how to do it!' Anxiety stems from uncertainty about the future and how to face it. By programming and reiterating that you'll be ready, your heart becomes hard and strong, and anxiety vanishes.

For Sadness, use the term: 'Surprise me!' Sadness often stems from a lack of novelty; a present that always seems the same eventually leads to depression. By focusing on what surprises you, whether it comes from you or your environment, your mood will improve, and you'll begin to appreciate even the smallest things because they surprise you.

Remember, the terms for programming should not feel like impositions. They should be set as proposals or suggestions, as if you were speaking to another person. This approach ensures that the process feels natural and conducive to your personal growth.

Through this practice, we learn to harness the power of breath as a vehicle for higher-level mental programming. We learn to let go of our anxieties and sadness, replacing them with the strength and surprise that emerge from deep within ourselves. This practice is more than a method; it's a path to a more mindful, balanced, and fulfilled life.

Creating Your Comfort Zone: The Black Sea

When you are alone, it's crucial to create your own comfort zone, a beautiful place to engage in enjoyable activities with wonderful people. This comfort zone doesn't necessarily have to be a physical space; it can also be a state of mind, a realm of memories and imagination where you find solace and joy.

Let's visualize this concept through a scenario I like to call "The Black Sea."

Picture a dark night on a beach with a pleasant temperature and a large yellow fire reaching up into the sky. Around this fire, gathered are all the people who matter to you, listening to you sing. Your hand strums a guitar, playing tunes by Bob Dylan, Johnny Cash, Hank Williams, and others. Your voice, accompanied by the guitar's melody, resonates in the night air, filling it with a harmonious rhythm.

One by one, more people join the group. They follow the music, their voices joining yours in song. Out of the darkness, your father joins, followed by relatives and friends with their respective partners. Your mother, Aunts and Uncles find their places around the fire, adding to the warmth of the gathering. Grandma and Cousin also join in, their faces illuminated by the flickering firelight. Lastly, from an unknown direction, the last person the have left life arrives, tall and silent, completing the circle around the fire.

There you are, all of you together, harmonizing with the sound of the sea serving as your backdrop. The crashing waves add a natural rhythm to your music, the salty air carrying your collective voices far into the night. The fire, the music, and the sea become a symphony, each component enhancing the others, creating a perfect moment of unity and joy.

In this scenario, you've successfully created a comfort zone in your mind, a place where you can retreat to whenever you feel the need for tranquillity and happiness. Remember, this comfort zone is not just a mere fantasy or an exercise in imagination. It's a representation of what you desire and value, a vision of perfect harmony, and a source of inspiration. It serves as a reminder that you have the power to create beautiful experiences and build meaningful connections. By visualizing and immersing yourself in such experiences, you are programming your mind to seek out and appreciate similar moments in your real life.

This is the essence of creating your comfort zone. It's about understanding what brings you joy and peace, and intentionally inviting those elements into your life. Whether it's through the companionship of loved ones, the soothing sound of the sea, or the joy of music, your comfort zone is a sanctuary where you can replenish your spirit and nurture your well-being.

The Observer Within

Have you ever noticed how consuming alcohol might make you feel like an observer of yourself? It creates a sense of detachment and indifference towards what comes next, with dulled senses and a feeling of lightness. This phenomenon provides an interesting insight into our self-perception and identity.

Indeed, your identity doesn't solely depend on your conscious self. There's a deeper ego within you that truly decides and acts. When you confuse this deeper ego with your conscious self, you end up carrying the weight of every decision and action on your shoulders.

However, in reality, you are an observer of yourself. You are the aura that surrounds and observes your actions and reactions, without necessarily being entangled in them. You don't need to worry excessively because your deeper self-manifests itself regardless of your anxieties.

Remember these key points:

- You are primarily an observer.

- Support your deeper ego, but realize it is something different and separate from your observing self.

This concept of being an observer can be a liberating perspective. It allows for a separation between the part of you that experiences emotions, thoughts, and actions, and the part of you that simply observes these experiences. It relieves the pressure of over-identification with every thought and action, leading to less self-judgment and more acceptance.

Furthermore, the observer within may be considered the only aspect of our consciousness that could persist beyond physical death. Why do we observe ourselves? The exact reasons might evade our understanding, but there are numerous clues hinting towards this intriguing aspect of human consciousness. By cultivating this observer perspective, we might not only improve our psychological well-being in the present but also gain insights into the nature of our existence and the mystery of consciousness itself.

People in Our Lives

It's a fact that during the day, especially for introverts, very little time is dedicated to thinking about the people around us. Our social relationships can suffer from this lack of attention, and this can, in turn, affect our mood.

It's important to focus individually on the people who are part of your life. They need to be nurtured and cared for, or unexpected things may occur that could disrupt your balance.

Every day, bring these people to mind. They represent your contact with the outside world and can, and should, support you. You cannot do everything from within your internal world. Others provide a source of positive energy that flows from the outside towards you.

Being mindful of the people in our lives doesn't mean obsessing over every social interaction, but rather acknowledging their existence and the roles they play in our lives. It's about appreciating their contributions, learning from the differences, and cultivating a sense of connection and community.

Remember, human beings are inherently social creatures. We thrive on connection and collaboration. By nurturing our relationships, we not only enhance our social lives but also foster our own personal growth and happiness. So, take a moment each day to consider the people who make up your world. This simple act could have a profound impact on your overall well-being and your understanding of your place in the world.

The Power of Visualization

It's a fact that most of the advice provided here, and the vast majority of your self-communication, is based on words, phrases, and concepts. But why does a rule for living better seem to lose its potency over time? This happens because words are no longer associated with an emotion and become emptied of their effectiveness. As emotional beings, we thrive on the potency of feelings. The ultimate goal is to communicate effectively with yourself and others.

The solution lies in using a language more suitable for self-communication, such as images and visualization.

* Make a habit of picturing in your mind what you want to tell yourself, without using words.

* Develop suggestions based on images, minimizing words just enough to keep things organized.

Consider how you teach your children. You aim to use few words, focusing first on creating an appropriate situation, and then you generate an image using various strategies.

Notice that when you can construct an image (a picture) with the person you're communicating with, they are often positively impacted. It's not just about what you say but also about how you paint a mental picture of it.

Endless writings can become tiresome, especially since they eventually need to be converted into images to be assimilated effectively. Thus, the power of visualization comes into play. Even if it's rough, draw your thoughts. Visualize them.

Visualization is a potent tool, allowing us to connect more deeply with our emotions, surpassing the limitations of words. It's a step towards more efficient self-communication and a healthier emotional state. It's not about disregarding words completely, but about finding a balance between verbal and visual communication, enhancing the overall process.

Remember, the most effective communication isn't always what's spoken or written. Sometimes, it's what's envisioned. Harness the power of visualization to enrich your self-communication and improve your life.

Multiple Worlds: Beyond Materialism and Stress

Life is full of stress, coming at us from different directions. Consider a scenario where you've been under immense stress from various sources, and finally, after a long time, you find yourself on a lengthy walk with your family.

Through your eyes, the world is heavily anchored in materialism and often borders on fatalism for various reasons. But that's not the whole story.

Our perception of the world, heavily rooted in materialism, is not the only reality. The truth is that not everything we see and feel is accurate. Scientific discoveries have time and again demonstrated that our senses are quite limited.

There are other worlds, other perspectives, and they interact with each other in different ways. Take, for instance, the world of energies and areas. This world is not about tangible objects, but rather about energies and fields. You can sense these energies as they envelop and interact with you and others.

The world of energies is just one of the different ways of perceiving things as they are. Explore more, as there will be various other perspectives, limited only by your imagination. But remember, these are not purely fantastical worlds. If you think about it, the world you see and hear is no less fantastic than others. After all, the eyes see only a few frequencies of light, and so it goes for sound and other senses.

You are blind if you only see the material world. It's not the only reality, and clinging to it may be why happiness seems elusive. The worlds are many, and you should not limit yourself to just one.

Your search should be continuous. Experiment, immerse yourself, and then search again. It's crucial to understand or verify the interactions between these worlds. Happiness lies here. Open your eyes!

Whether these multiple universes truly exist or not is somewhat irrelevant. The positive effect on the brain is evident, akin to a tipsy person feeling better by dulling their senses: the mind opens, expands, and becomes serene.

In this journey of exploration and discovery, remember to balance the various worlds you inhabit. Take the time to appreciate the energies around you and remember that there is more to life than the material world. It's in these moments that you may find the happiness you seek.

The Power of Now: Living in the Present

As human beings, we often find ourselves contemplating the past or projecting into the future. The past can be a comforting memory, lulling us to sleep with thoughts of things that have happened. The future, on the other hand, is filled with uncertainties, tasks to accomplish, and challenges that may not be entirely desirable.

The Future

Living in the future can create anxiety. We envision all the possible problems, and even when there are no particular problems at hand, we feel anxious about those that could occur without warning. This constant apprehension and worry about what lies ahead can cloud our present, robbing us of the joy of the moment.

The Past

Living in the past, conversely, can lead to depression. It's enjoyable to revisit the things that have happened to us: the events, the people, the places we've seen and visited with great emotion, the loves, the conquests, the challenges. But this constant dwelling in the past creates a disconnect with the present. The present doesn't have these characteristics, and when you inevitably have to return to it, you may feel overwhelmed, wanting to close your eyes.

There's a phenomenon akin to that of a retired police officer who, after witnessing so many things, ends up taking his own life. This person lives in the past, constantly and exclusively. The present disconcerts them, annihilates them, and depresses them to the point of suicide. This is a stark reminder of how dwelling too much in the past can lead to feelings of hopelessness.

The Present

It's clear that living in the present fosters a more positive attitude, even if it may not seem so at first glance. If you strive to live in the "now", moment by moment, without projecting yourself into time (and therefore space), you will gradually find pleasure in existing, in seeing, and in appreciating even the smallest things.

But be cautious. Immersing yourself in the present requires a strong and vivid projection. It's easy to fall back into the past without realizing it, or into the future. Maintaining awareness and mindfulness is key to remaining present.

The challenge is to balance our relationship with time. Remembering the past, planning for the future, and living in the present are all important aspects of life. However, the real key to happiness and peace lies in finding joy in the present moment, for it's the only time we truly have.

Inner Communication: Rationality versus Sensations

Your "self" doesn't always communicate effectively with rationality. The subconscious isn't accessible through rational activities, but through sensations. It's essential to project these sensations and communicate with your inner self in this manner. Study this mode of communication, expand it, and make it efficient.

This explains why any meditation technique can fail. When it no longer evokes or recalls emotions, it fails to communicate with your subconscious. Or to put it in another way, sensations must be evoked by these techniques. If the techniques fail, they need to be changed or updated to evoke the necessary emotions for making contact with, influencing, and communicating with the subconscious.

It's undeniable that all the techniques developed so far have their reason for being. They simply need to be understood from a reverse perspective.

Emotion can be projected from the outside or from within. Focus more on the external projection of emotion because, given your nature, it's the one you lack the most. External emotions can come from various sources such as interactions with others, experiences in nature, or the consumption of art and culture. Try to identify the external sources that effectively stimulate your emotions, and incorporate them into your daily life.

Remember, the goal isn't to suppress rationality but to find a balance between your rational thoughts and emotional sensations. Both play a vital role in shaping your experiences and navigating the world. The key is to foster a harmonious dialogue between these two aspects of your psyche.

Discovering Self-Value: the Job Interview effect

It's observed that during a job interview and the subsequent phase, my value in unexpected sectors, such as the human and relational ones, is significant, much higher than average and even more than what you thought of myself. After interviews like these, you immediately feel much more confident, strong, and sure that you are doing the right thing. It's not just about deserving a higher place in society than what you currently occupy. If we want, my intelligence is far above average, especially in how you manage to perceive, reflect, and reprocess details that others miss.

It's incredible how important interaction is for someone who avoids it by nature. A strategy to enhance, develop, and make the most of this side of myself is needed, but it's difficult. You must find a way to interact with others on a regular basis, even though you find it stressful.

I keep reflecting on what you have said and brought up with other people, you reprocess it a bit, and you are pleased with this persona. you like his acumen. You, who have never had an idol after my father, find yourself idolizing yourself. It's only noticeable when this character interacts with others, focuses, and manifests himself.

It's something that isn't noticed, and in the logic of the continuous search to always stay on top, it's important.

You are the idol you wish to be. It's absurd but not an excess of pathetic stubbornness; it's true. This character is noteworthy, and you like him.

The level of confidence reached after the interview and the continuous rethinking of your speeches is such that you don't care if you passed the interview (the result hasn't been communicated yet). you'll succeed in another circumstance because, in some ways, you're a genius. It's absurd, but true!

At this point, the question arises: what kind of genius are you? One who manages to perceive, reprocess, and find improvement ideas in the most disparate sectors is the result of a mix of abilities, and not just one specific skill.

Harnessing and Maximizing Your Energy: A Guide to Training Consistency"

It's a well-known fact, but it's worth articulating to solidify the understanding once and for all. It's undeniable that especially during the training of combat sports, one experiences a kind of energy wave. In other words, there are periods of high energy and periods of low energy. Obviously, when energy is low, one may struggle to get to the gym for a variety of reasons, but ultimately it always comes down to energy levels. If you pay attention, you can predict in advance whether you'll make it to the gym next time or not. The awareness of this fact should bring peace of mind that it's not possible to be consistent in training at all times.

So, how can we make the positive wave last as long as possible? Having a clear VISION of where you want to go with that specific training in the near future can certainly be a great help, but it's something that we have always struggled with and haven't found lasting methods to extend the positive wave.

It's likely something perceived from the intensity of the last workout or the impending work activities that consume a lot of energy, as well as a mere hormonal fact. It's very likely that it's a mix of these factors.

"There's an Energy Wave for physical activities, perceive it and improve it."

Physical activity is a healthful behaviour that has promise for combating feelings of fatigue and low energy. All of the studies suggest that there's an association between physical activity and a reduced risk of experiencing feelings of low energy and fatigue when active adults are compared with sedentary peers 【47†source】 .

To enhance stamina and prolong high-energy periods in physical activity, one can follow many different strategies all linked with sporting activities.

It's important to remember that everyone is unique, and what works for one person might not work for another. Experiment with different strategies and find what helps you extend your periods of high energy the most effectively. Also, remember that low-energy periods are normal and part of the training cycle. Use these periods for rest and recovery so that you can come back stronger and more energized for your next training session.

Understanding your energy levels and how they fluctuate can be crucial for your training regimen. By employing methods to extend the positive wave, you can better harness your energy and make the most out of your workouts. Just remember, the key is to listen to your body and respect its needs. It's not about being perfect; it's about progress and improvement.

Harnessing the Power of Vision

In all of my progress in work and life, a common thread has been prevalent, even in minor events: having a vision of what you want to happen. Envisioning a rough sketch of the events you want to happen, always based on achievable things, is a powerful technique that predisposes your entire being towards the desired event. It is also undeniable that this leads to a certain connection with the world around you and even to a certain luck. There's a significant difference between a vision and a dream. A dream often has no basis for realization and is often self-contained and usually doesn't materialize. A vision, on the other hand, has a real basis and creates a predisposition not only mentally but also spiritually to the event.

The characteristics of a vision include:

1) It is based on a realizable event, not just a dream, and is connected with a deep and intimate desire of yours.

2) It is generally a high-level sketch or program, as the details will emerge when the conditions present themselves, but in its sketch, there may also be some details.

3) It must be repeated, like a mantra. Its effectiveness increases with repetition.

4) The vision is not static.

a. It must be refined and filled with some details as the vision becomes clearer and less sketchy, although it remains a rough plan.

b. It is only limited by your imagination, although tied to the real world, it can expand to possibilities that one cannot imagine.

The effectiveness of the vision is not in question, also because there are many writings about it, direct and indirect, mine and not. A side effect of the vision is the creation of states of ecstasy and mental alteration, which are generally positive.

When you make a mental master plan or put it in writing, you are simply visualizing what you want to do. It is clear that planning is beneficial because it gives you a vision of the desired event.

Seeing the Bigger Picture

Vision gives you a complete view of upcoming events without getting lost and terrified by the details of daily life. Notice that depression strikes especially when you do not have an overall vision and you get lost in living daily events. Always projecting the complete vision of what you do projected in time and space not only concentrates your forces in the desired direction but also fights the depression of daily living. In other words, it is necessary to distract attention from the countless daily activities and duties (annoying), and the best method is to stay focused on the overall vision.

When to Project the Vision

• One of the best times is during solitary walks in a relaxing environment, you are more easily inspired.

• Another occasion is when you go to bed early and have time before falling asleep, it is difficult to fall asleep when you develop visions, so it is not suitable if you go to bed late.

Reinforcing Visions

• Writing down a couple of lines about the visions that interest you are the best way to reinforce them. Doing everything always in mind can be misleading. What is written is not necessarily to be taken literally, it is a way to reorganize and strengthen the ideas associated with the visions susceptible to variations and updates. It is important that the writing is descriptive of the vision.

• Images that synthesize concepts and reinforce the visual, vision is a visual projection, so it works very well with images (take them from the internet for ease and modify them).

The Rainfall of Fortune

Close your eyes for a moment and visualize what you truly desire, without fear. Fixate on the idea that, to achieve your dream, luck plays a significant role. It's not merely about the actions you initiate. Being overly focused on the actions you need to take to attain your desire can create stress, as it seems like an insurmountable task. But it isn't so. You must recognize that luck serves as the foundation of your success, followed by actions. Primarily, stay focused on luck.

Don't worry about the future. Luck is the principal resource. Your role is merely to act in harmony with fortunate events. You can stimulate such lucky incidents with simple activities like persistently asking questions, investigating, and seeking information.

Luck doesn't originate from you; it doesn't revolve around self-concentration. Instead, it thrives on your focus on the environment surrounding you. The more you pay attention to people, situations, and the places where you find yourself, the more luck will smile upon you.

Think of the games of chance you play. You win far more easily when you're not solely focused on yourself but rather on the people you're playing with and the environment. Why is that so? Is it a psychological phenomenon or something else? It's hard to say.

Remember that you're striving to achieve something, but the path is intricate and challenging. It depends on many of your actions, and the plan has various aspects that aren't under your control.

But don't forget, a touch of luck is required. Luck comes on its own. It presents itself more readily if you're connected with the environment rather than being isolated within yourself. An auspicious event always occurs to rescue you and make things easier. Therefore, don't be overly tense. For certain events, remember: a bit of luck is necessary.

Luck will come right on time, perhaps in an unexpected form, but it will arrive.

This chapter is a reminder that while hard work and dedication are vital in achieving our goals, sometimes, it's the unpredictable sprinkle of luck that completes the picture. It's not something we can control or guarantee, but it's something we can welcome with open arms when it does arrive. So, let's keep our eyes and minds open, embrace the world around us, and be ready to seize the opportunities when fortune decides to rain down upon us.

The Momentum of Progress

It may seem like a self-evident remark, yet we often overlook its truth: keep moving. This mantra is more than just a reminder to stay active—it's a philosophy, a way of life, a driver of progress.

Life is a continuum of learning and growing, and stagnation is its antithesis. So, venture into the unknown. Experiment with new things, request enhancements, enrol in courses. Begin new projects, take that leap of faith. Even if you don't succeed at first, the experience will bring its own rewards. It will teach you resilience, broaden your perspective, and endow you with knowledge that may prove indispensable in the future.

Movement is synonymous with life. It breathes vitality into your existence and uplifts your mood. When you're actively pursuing your goals, you're not just existing—you're living. But remember, it's not always about the destination; the journey itself holds invaluable lessons and experiences.

You might be waiting for success to come knocking, and it's easy to get disheartened when it doesn't show up as quickly as you'd like. But don't let this dampen your spirits. Keep in mind that success isn't always instant. It's often the result of persistent effort, patience, and a multitude of attempts. Each step you take, each risk you embrace, brings you closer to your goals.

Keep moving, even when the odds seem to be stacked against you. Even when you feel like you're running into dead ends. Even when the road ahead seems steep and uncertain. It's the very act of moving that gives you strength and resilience.

In the grand scheme of life, each step you take, no matter how small, contributes to your journey. Each experience, whether perceived as good or bad, shapes you and propels you forward.

Remember, it's not about the speed at which you move; it's about maintaining the momentum, no matter how slow or how fast. It's about the perseverance to keep trying, the determination to keep learning, the courage to keep exploring.

This chapter is a reminder that the road to success is often paved with trials and errors, but it's the constant movement that eventually leads you there. It's only a matter of time and the number of attempts. So, keep moving.

The Power of Novelty

New rules, new paths, new experiences—these are the elements that bring a spark of novelty into our lives. Initially, they strike us with an emotional impact, providing a fresh perspective and eliciting excitement. However, over time, we adapt to these changes and they become rationalized, losing their once transformative power. That's when the need for newer, slightly different rules arises.

The ability to creatively introduce novelty into your life, particularly in the everyday mundane, can be an invigorating experience. This doesn't mean you need to make drastic changes; sometimes, the smallest shifts in routine can expose you to the unexpected and bring about a sense of wonder.

Consider this: instead of your usual walk to work or the supermarket, embark on an aimless outdoor stroll. Breathe in the fresh air deeply, let your thoughts wander, and allow your feelings to be captured by the subtle novelties around you. A new alleyway might present unseen sights, triggering fresh thoughts and inspiration. This new energy can be a beneficial tool for your work and mood alike.

Try your hand at learning a new musical instrument, delve into a genre of books you've never explored before. Each new endeavour should be approached with a healthy dose of creativity, rather than being a repetitive, rigidly framed action.

Reflecting back to my personal journey, I recall a shift from 1997 to 1998. My world, once based on sensing the intangible, abruptly came to a halt. I believe this happened simply because I lost my creativity towards novelty; the introduction of the new. Everything started feeling repetitive, and things began to malfunction. That's the logic of the mind—it craves novelty, always something slightly different, introducing new things that inspire before the current ones cease to take effect.

Indeed, when this works, it feels as invigorating as a drug. You're filled with a zeal for life, a desire to do and achieve. However, much like a drug, the effect fades over time and you need something new and different to rekindle the feeling. So, embrace the power of novelty, infuse your life with new experiences and watch as it fuels your creativity, passion, and overall zest for life.

The Ebb and Flow of Rules

Are rules ephemeral? The context in which they are applied may suggest so.

Indeed, context is a fundamental element when discussing rules. The validity of a rule is tied to a well-defined external and internal environment. You may apply a rule effectively, but eventually, the external environment changes, often beyond your control, and this shift influences you too.

As an example, consider a period of your life characterized by calm and minimal stress. During such times, you might apply rules such as practicing meditation or introspective self-exploration. However, if the context changes—say you start feeling lonely or restless—this change reflects on the rules you're applying. Little by little, they lose their effectiveness.

This does not mean the rules become obsolete. When the context aligns again, these rules can function perfectly well. This highlights the importance of recognizing the context in which you are living, and for which the rule you wish to apply is relevant.

Contextual shifts are a part of life. They represent the natural ebb and flow of circumstances, emotions, and experiences. Recognizing these changes and adapting your rulebook accordingly is essential. Understanding the context in which a rule is applied allows you to use it more effectively and adjust as necessary when things change.

It's crucial to remember that a rule's efficacy is not solely determined by its intrinsic worth but also by the environment in which it operates. Just as a fish thrives in water but struggles on land, so too do rules work best when applied in the right context. So, the next time you find a rule losing its effect, instead of discarding it outright, consider if it's the rule that's flawed or simply the context that's changed.

The Conscious Filter and the Pursuit of Happiness

Your conscious mind acts as a filter for your sensations, influencing your behaviour. When this filter is too robust, your brain is perpetually seeking problems to solve, either in the future or even dredging up issues from the past. This overactive problem-solving can turn into a relentless hunt for critical elements, creating a constant state of tension.

The key is to appropriately relax this filter, enabling the brain to focus more on sensations. In this state, our perception of time can fade away. After all, time is an abstract concept; only the present moment truly exists in the sensory world.

Interestingly, alcohol has a similar effect: it reduces the filter, allowing more sensations to reach the brain. However, if used excessively, the lack of a filter can lead to behaviour that is not socially acceptable. As in many things, moderation is key.

Visualize the filter as a wall full of holes. The challenge lies in recognizing when the filter is overly intense, and adjusting accordingly. When the filter is too potent, it can lead to increased anxiety and stress. Being able to notice this overactivity and manage it is an essential skill.

Happiness is not a state but a process. It's a journey rather than a destination. The goal is not to arrive at a static state of joy but to continually move through life, experiencing the full range of emotions, learning, growing, and ultimately, finding happiness in the journey itself.

Remember, the goal is not to remove the filter entirely, but to learn to adjust it according to the demands of your current situation. This conscious adjustment of your mental filter allows you to fully experience the present moment, reducing anxiety and stress, and paving the way for a happier, more fulfilled life. Keep moving and find your happiness.

Harnessing Brain Power for Optimal Work Performance

One of the most effective ways to prepare your brain for work and critical activities is to begin contemplating your tasks immediately upon waking. This strategy relies on the understanding that the first thing the brain focuses on upon waking tends to occupy its attention throughout the day. By directing your thoughts toward your work first thing in the morning, you can potentially enhance your productivity and performance.

This technique can be practiced over several days. However, be mindful of the consequences. This intense concentration can channel your energy towards your work goals but, if not carefully managed, it may also lead to increased stress levels. Your brain might become overly focused on work, leaving little room for relaxation or other important aspects of life. This kind of mental overdrive can lead to burnout if not properly balanced.

Therefore, after a few days of utilizing this strategy, it is advisable to take a break when the opportunity arises. Allow your brain to switch off from work and focus on other subjects. This could involve engaging in a hobby, spending time with loved ones, exercising, or simply enjoying some quiet time. The goal is to provide a much-needed respite for your brain and to create a healthier work-life balance.

Upon waking, resist the urge to immediately think about work or tasks for the day. If your mind naturally drifts towards work, gently guide it towards an alternative subject. This strategy can help to reduce stress levels and promote a more relaxed and balanced state of mind. Remember, your brain is a powerful tool, but it also needs time to rest and recharge. Manage your mental energy wisely, and you'll find your days can become more productive and less stressful.

The Art of Effective Interactions: Psychology Tricks for Relationships

Navigating the intricate landscape of interpersonal interactions can sometimes be daunting. Whether you're in a high-stakes meeting, navigating social gatherings, or simply trying to establish a bond with someone new, understanding the psychology of relationships can be an invaluable tool. This chapter will delve into several relationship tricks, providing a deeper understanding of their workings and showing how they can be applied effectively.

1. The Power of Eye Contact

Imagine a situation where you've asked a question, but the answer you receive leaves you unsatisfied or confused. In such a scenario, instead of rephrasing or asking a different question, try maintaining eye contact. This non-verbal action can create a sense of pressure, compelling the person to elaborate on their thoughts. It's a subtle tactic that draws upon the human instinct to clarify and resolve ambiguity when under scrutiny.

2. Strategic Positioning

Sometimes, we find ourselves sharing a space with aggressive individuals. It might be a tough client at a meeting or a difficult person at a social gathering. In such instances, an effective strategy can be to sit next to the aggressor. While it might feel uncomfortable initially, the close proximity can actually diffuse the level of aggression. This happens for a few reasons: it forces them to physically turn towards you, it introduces an intimidation factor, and it makes the conversation more personal, removing the opportunity to hide within the group's circle.

3. The Relief of Writing

In times of stress or anxiety, a simple yet effective trick is to write down your thoughts. The act of putting pen to paper and expressing your concerns can serve as an emotional release, reducing the mental burden you carry. It's akin to sharing your thoughts with someone, thereby creating a sense of relief that allows you to focus more effectively on your tasks.

4. The Disarming Question

The next time you find yourself being verbally attacked, try responding with, "Are you okay?" This unexpected question can shift the dynamics of the interaction, causing the aggressor to pause and potentially defuse the situation. By redirecting the conversation, the other person is put in a position where they have to consider their own state of mind, disrupting the cycle of blame and aggression.

5. The Art of Asking for Help

When in need of assistance, start the conversation with, "I need your help..." This phrase does two things: it makes the person feel needed and useful, and it subtly plays on their dislike for feeling guilty. This strategic way of asking increases the likelihood of receiving the help you need.

6. Optimum Eye Contact

Eye contact can be a powerful tool for creating a friendly and confident impression. During introductions, try making a mental note of the person's eye colour. The exercise of noting their eye colour ensures that you maintain a solid few seconds of eye contact, which can help establish a positive connection.

7. The Yawning Test

Have you ever felt someone's gaze on you and wondered if they were indeed watching you? Here's a simple trick to confirm your suspicion: Yawn. After yawning, quickly glance at the person. If they yawn too, chances are they were watching you. This happens because yawning is contagious and often subconsciously triggers a yawn in the observer.

8. Make a Request Too Large to Fulfil

This is a classic psychological trick known as the Door-in-the-face technique. If you want someone to do something for you, start by asking for something significantly larger than what you actually need. When they refuse, as expected, make your real request. The person you're asking will likely feel a sense of relief that your new request is much smaller, and will be more inclined to help. This technique takes advantage of the principle of reciprocity; when you make a concession by lowering your request, the other person will feel obliged to make a concession in return, which often means agreeing to your proposal.

9. Teach to Learn

If you're trying to learn something new, one of the most effective methods is to teach the material to someone else. It may seem counterintuitive, especially if you're still trying to master the content yourself, but the process of teaching forces you to understand the topic on a deeper level. When you have to explain a concept to someone else, you need to make sure you've fully grasped it yourself. Furthermore, when you receive questions or feedback, you're given the opportunity to view the topic from different perspectives, which can deepen your understanding even further.

10. Use Affinity to Build Trust

Building trust is a key aspect of any relationship, and a technique called 'affinity' can aid in this process. Affinity refers to a sense of familiarity or comfort that comes from frequent interaction or exposure. The more 'present' you are in someone's life, the more familiar you become, and the more trust they tend to have in you. So, if you're looking to establish a strong bond with someone, try to increase your presence in their life. This could mean spending more time with them, frequently checking in, or simply being there when they need you.

11. Chew Gum to Calm Nerves

Nervousness and anxiety can often set in before an important event. Instead of succumbing to these feelings, try chewing gum. This may seem like a simple act, but it can have a profound impact on your nervous system. Our brains are wired to associate eating with safety and comfort. So, when you chew gum, your brain interprets this action as a sign that you're safe, which can help to alleviate feelings of worry and nervousness.

Remember, these tricks are not fool proof, and they should be used responsibly, with respect for the autonomy and feelings of others. They are meant to improve communication and understanding, not to manipulate others for personal gain. Use them wisely, and you may find that they can help you navigate the complexities of social interaction with greater ease and confidence.

Embracing the Depths Within

The preceding chapters have led us towards a newly formulated concept that can be both intriguing and challenging: learning to live and be what is not immediately apparent on the surface. This means not only communicating with the subconscious but becoming the subconscious. It's an odd proposition, one that might even seem absurd or insane out of context, yet it is precisely what practitioners of meditation strive to do on a daily basis.

Of course, our daily activities demand that we operate on a higher, more conscious level. Tasks need to be completed, responsibilities need to be fulfilled. Yet, our endeavour, as ambitious as it may sound, is to literally become what we are at a deeper, less accessible level. This lower level may seem alien to us, yet it is an integral part of our being.

As we move forward, it is important to understand that this is not about negating or neglecting our conscious, thinking selves. Instead, it is about a deeper integration, a harmonious balance that allows the conscious and subconscious to work together, informing and enriching each other.

The journey towards this deeper level of self-understanding and self-realization is not a straightforward or easy one. It demands patience, discipline, and a willingness to venture into the unknown. It calls for a willingness to embrace ambiguity and uncertainty, to be open to the surprises and revelations that may surface along the way.

One might question, why undertake this journey at all? The answer lies in the potential rewards it offers. By embracing our subconscious selves, we stand to gain a richer, fuller understanding of who we are. We open ourselves to insights and realizations that can transform our perspectives and our approach to life. We cultivate a sense of inner peace and equanimity that can serve as a steadying force amid the ups and downs of daily existence.

In the following chapters, we will delve more deeply into how we can begin to bridge the gap between the conscious and the subconscious. We will explore techniques and practices that can help us tune in to our subconscious selves, including various forms of meditation. We will also examine the challenges that may arise on this journey and how we can navigate them effectively.

In embarking on this journey, it is important to remember that there is no 'right' or 'wrong' way to proceed. Each of us is unique, and what works for one person may not work for another. The key is to approach this journey with an open mind, a compassionate heart, and a spirit of curiosity and exploration. With these qualities as our guide, we can look forward to a journey of self-discovery that is both deeply personal and profoundly transformative.

The Power of Positive Projection

Your mind has the remarkable ability to manifest in your life what it consumes. This concept is rooted in the understanding that our thoughts, feelings, and beliefs significantly influence our reality. If you constantly consume unpleasant sensations or negative thoughts, your mind will project them into your life, amplifying negativity.

Conversely, if you focus on projecting positive thoughts and emotions, you will start to notice more positivity in your life. It's a process of magnifying the positive, highlighting it in your conscious awareness, and seeking it out actively. It's like adjusting the lens through which you view your world.

However, it's important to recognize that negative thoughts and emotions are a part of human nature. There will be moments when your mind starts to project scenes of despair, negativity, or violence. During these moments, it's crucial not to let your mind dwell on these harmful projections. Instead, seek distraction, engage in positive activities, or practice mindfulness.

In essence, make conscious efforts to redirect your focus towards positive elements. While it may seem challenging initially, with consistent practice, your mind will gradually shift towards positivity. This shift won't eliminate negative thoughts entirely but will help you manage them better, enabling you to lead a more balanced and fulfilling life.

Remember, your mind is a powerful tool that shapes your reality. It's your responsibility to feed it with positivity, kindness, and optimism to create a more positive and fulfilling life experience. The power of positive projection is in your hands. Use it wisely.

The Power of the Pen - Overcoming the Wave of Emptiness

Have you ever experienced days when you felt entirely empty, devoid of any capability to interact with your world pleasantly, and yet you couldn't pinpoint why? Especially when, in general, you're a person brimming with creativity, vigour, and strength. This chapter offers a suggestion for transcending this wave-like effect of emptiness.

Writing is often recommended in literature as a method to cultivate calmness and establish a balance with oneself. Let's delve deeper into this concept.

When you engage in creative writing, you're indirectly stimulating your subconscious, enabling you to create, connect, and express what has been deeply repressed within you. Even though it's a high-level activity, if you focus more on the underlying concepts rather than the mere technique of writing, you will remain constantly inspired throughout your day.

Throughout the typical day, you won't just be in the room or the place where you are. There's always a vast, creative space within you, filled with exciting unpredictability, and it's in your story. Writing stories is the best way to program or, better yet, stimulate your subconscious. It should be noted that writing technical articles or books also helps, but to a slightly lesser degree. However, if the creative activity within the story itself doesn't end when you put down the pen, you'll experience the world around you with greater lightness and fullness.

You'll find yourself, much like after an extended meditation session, detached and alert, easily resolving the day-to-day unpredictability's. The beauty lies within your mind, you develop it, and then you fix it on paper (or any other medium). You'll realize that the story is a reflection of you, and even if you don't publish it, you have anchored a part of yourself.

Write stories and books consistently and creatively, even multiple ones at a time. Plan writings, create indexes and plots for future development. As already mentioned, do it in a non-systematic way, because the subconscious works better when it's free to hop from topic to topic, subject to subject. Every moment, every day, develop the plots of your stories.

The more you develop your stories, the deeper and more connected you become with yourself. You start to develop concepts that go well beyond the mere story you're writing.

This activity can easily be extended to painting and drawing. It's the constant creative activity that allows you to transcend yourself, always and at every moment of your day. By understanding and harnessing the power of the written word, you can navigate the wave of emptiness, transforming it into a source of profound self-discovery and creative expression.

The Ultimate Question: Happiness

The primary target of your entire life is: to be Happy.

Please note that we're discussing complete happiness here, the kind that is attained in all the fields that you enjoy, that provide pleasure and completeness, hence, it is meant in a very broad sense.

The question you should pose to your subconscious during most hours of the day is: "How can I be happy at every moment?" Notice that there's a temporal aspect to this question, asking you to focus on the present.

The effect of feeling happy is warmth in your chest, a muted sense of contentment simply from looking around you. It's like a castle that wraps around and protects you, even from the harshest circumstances, because why can't you be happy now, without waiting!

The answers I've obtained so far include:

1. Music (listening to it, playing it, and experiencing it)

2. Observing the small things around you, there's always something you like (a colour, an object, a person...)

3. Humour, laughing even at yourself brings joy.

Happiness is a goal, a journey, and a destination all at once. It is not always the grand events or significant milestones that bring us the most joy. Often, it is the little things, the small moments, the minor victories that can make us feel truly happy.

So, pose this question to yourself frequently, "How can I be happy at every moment?" and explore the multitude of ways you can cultivate happiness in your life. The answers might surprise you, but they will certainly guide you on your path to a more fulfilled and joyous existence.

Conclusion

As the author of this book, I am applying the methods described herein while writing. Particularly, I am practicing a light version of meditation aimed at elevating the spirit, which should be performed at least once a day, though twice or thrice is recommended. This consists of thirty rapid breaths in a quiet, outdoor environment, followed by slowing down of the breath and projecting a connection with the external world, feeling the wind and the sound of the birds.

During the day, especially in moments of high emotional stress, visualizing the "black pool" is helpful to understand the true state of the subconscious. The simple awareness of the state of the subconscious can bring calm. Remain with this vision for a while.

Repeating your short-form name thirty times helps to distract the mind from its constant search for something to think about. It empties the mind and connects a lower level of consciousness. This repetition can be performed for 2 or 3 cycles in sequence. Remember that the use of the term, in this case, your name, is just a word. The concept to aim for is to repeat to yourself everything you are in every sense; this is rightly identified with your name for brevity, but this is what you should strive for.

Developing the plot of stories, planning new books, is an activity that is not forced. Simply prepare for the development of the books that you usually write in the evening. There is no need to define a minimum number of words, but generally writing no less than 500 words per day is useful. If you are preparing the table of contents for a new book, the number of words is significantly reduced, but the creative activity is much higher than that usually used to write the daily 500 words. In other words, writing in itself is not necessary; what is essential is to keep the creative activity at the centre of your day.

You will realize that you are not a trivial person at all. The depth of your thoughts is enormous, your thirst for knowledge is vast, and your dynamism is exceptional.

Notes: